EMMANUEL JOSEPH

The Consideration of Abandonment,
Strategic Exits from Failing Markets
Without Moral Collapse

Copyright © 2025 by Emmanuel Joseph

All rights reserved. No part of this publication may be reproduced, stored or transmitted in any form or by any means, electronic, mechanical, photocopying, recording, scanning, or otherwise without written permission from the publisher. It is illegal to copy this book, post it to a website, or distribute it by any other means without permission.

First edition

This book was professionally typeset on Reedsy. Find out more at reedsy.com

Contents

1. Chapter 1 — 1
2. Chapter 1: The Dilemma of Departure — 3
3. Chapter 2: The Anatomy of a Failing Market — 5
4. Chapter 3: Stakeholders and the Weight of Responsibility — 8
5. Chapter 4: The Moral Case for Strategic Exits — 10
6. Chapter 5: Crafting an Ethical Exit Strategy — 11
7. Chapter 6: The Role of Communication in Ethical Exits — 13
8. Chapter 7: The Aftermath of Abandonment — 14
9. Chapter 8: Learning from Failure — 15
10. Chapter 9: Building Resilience for Future Challenges — 16
11. Chapter 10: The Global Perspective on Market Exits — 17
12. Chapter 11: The Future of Ethical Exits — 18
13. Chapter 12: A Call to Ethical Action — 19
14. Epilogue: The Ripple Effect of Ethical Choices — 20

1

Chapter 1

Introduction to *The Invisible Market: Monetizing the Untapped Potential of Non-Monetary Economies*

In a world driven by financial transactions and profit margins, there exists a vast, often overlooked realm where value is created and exchanged without the exchange of money. This is the invisible market—a space where barter systems, community sharing, volunteer work, and other non-monetary economies thrive. *The Invisible Market* seeks to uncover the hidden potential of these systems, exploring how they can be understood, leveraged, and even monetized in ways that benefit individuals, businesses, and societies at large. This book is an invitation to rethink what we consider valuable and to see opportunity where others see only absence.

The invisible market is not a new concept; it has existed for centuries, often operating in the shadows of formal economies. From the exchange of goods and services in rural communities to the digital barter systems emerging in online spaces, these non-monetary economies have sustained livelihoods and fostered connections in ways that traditional markets cannot. Yet, despite their ubiquity and resilience, they remain understudied and undervalued. This book aims to change that, offering a comprehensive exploration of how these systems work, why they matter, and how they can be integrated into mainstream economic thinking.

At its heart, *The Invisible Market* challenges the assumption that value must always be tied to currency. It argues that non-monetary economies are not just alternatives to traditional markets but are essential components of a holistic economic ecosystem. By examining real-world examples—from time banks and skill-sharing networks to collaborative consumption platforms—the book demonstrates how these systems create value in ways that go beyond financial gain. They build trust, strengthen communities, and provide access to resources for those who might otherwise be excluded from the formal economy.

But this book is not just an academic exploration; it is a practical guide for those looking to tap into the potential of non-monetary economies. Whether you are a business leader seeking innovative ways to engage with customers, a policymaker aiming to support underserved communities, or an individual looking to make the most of your skills and resources, *The Invisible Market* offers actionable insights and strategies. It provides a roadmap for identifying opportunities, building partnerships, and creating sustainable models that bridge the gap between monetary and non-monetary systems.

Ultimately, *The Invisible Market* is a call to expand our understanding of what it means to create and exchange value. It invites readers to look beyond the visible, to see the richness of human ingenuity and collaboration that exists outside traditional economic frameworks. In a time of growing inequality and environmental challenges, this book offers a hopeful vision of how we can harness the power of non-monetary economies to build a more inclusive, resilient, and equitable world. The invisible market is all around us—it's time to bring it into the light.

2

Chapter 1: The Dilemma of Departure

In the world of business, the decision to exit a failing market is rarely straightforward. Companies often find themselves torn between financial survival and ethical responsibility. The first chapter introduces the concept of strategic abandonment, exploring the tension between profit-driven decisions and the moral obligations businesses have to their employees, customers, and communities. It sets the stage for a deeper examination of how companies can navigate these complex choices without sacrificing their integrity.

The chapter delves into historical examples of market exits, both successful and disastrous, to illustrate the consequences of poorly managed departures. It highlights the importance of foresight, planning, and empathy in making such decisions. The narrative emphasizes that abandonment is not inherently unethical, but the manner in which it is executed can determine whether a company emerges with its reputation intact or tarnished.

A key theme introduced here is the idea of "moral collapse"—the point at which a company's actions during an exit erode trust and goodwill irreparably. The chapter argues that avoiding this collapse requires a balance between pragmatism and principle. It challenges readers to consider the broader implications of their decisions, urging them to think beyond short-term gains.

The chapter concludes by posing a central question: Can a company exit a failing market in a way that is both strategic and ethical? This question serves as the foundation for the rest of the book, inviting readers to explore the nuanced solutions and frameworks that follow.

3

Chapter 2: The Anatomy of a Failing Market

In the early 2000s, a mid-sized electronics manufacturer, *BrightTech*, found itself at the forefront of the booming market for portable CD players. For years, the company thrived, riding the wave of consumer demand for compact, on-the-go music devices. However, by the mid-2000s, cracks began to appear in the market. The rise of MP3 players, followed swiftly by smartphones, signaled a seismic shift in consumer preferences. BrightTech, once a leader in its niche, was suddenly facing declining sales, shrinking profit margins, and an uncertain future.

At first, BrightTech's leadership dismissed the warning signs. They attributed the dip in sales to temporary market fluctuations and doubled down on their existing product line, investing heavily in marketing campaigns and minor product upgrades. The company's executives were confident that their loyal customer base would sustain them through what they believed was a passing trend. However, as months turned into years, it became clear that the decline was not temporary. Competitors who had pivoted to digital music technology were thriving, while BrightTech's sales continued to plummet.

The turning point came when BrightTech's largest retail partner, a major electronics chain, announced it would no longer carry portable CD players due to lack of consumer interest. This was a devastating blow, as the retailer accounted for nearly 40% of BrightTech's revenue. Around the same time, suppliers began raising prices, citing decreased demand for CD player components. Caught between shrinking revenues and rising costs, BrightTech was forced to lay off a significant portion of its workforce. Morale within the company hit an all-time low, and the once-vibrant culture of innovation gave way to a sense of resignation and defeat.

BrightTech's story is a textbook example of a failing market. The company failed to recognize the early signs of disruption, clinging to outdated technology and underestimating the speed at which consumer preferences were changing. By the time leadership acknowledged the severity of the situation, it was too late to pivot effectively. The company's delayed response not only resulted in financial losses but also damaged its reputation, making it harder to recover in the long term.

This case study underscores the importance of understanding the anatomy of a failing market. BrightTech's downfall was not inevitable; it was the result of a series of missteps rooted in denial, poor strategic planning, and a lack of foresight. By examining where BrightTech went wrong, this chapter aims to provide readers with the tools to identify and respond to market decline before it's too late. The lessons from BrightTech's experience are clear: recognizing the signs of a failing market early, embracing change, and acting decisively are essential for survival in an ever-evolving business landscape.

Not all failing markets are created equal. This chapter examines the various factors that contribute to a market's decline, from economic shifts and technological disruptions to regulatory changes and consumer behavior. It provides a detailed framework for identifying the signs of a failing market, helping businesses recognize when it might be time to consider an exit.

The chapter also explores the emotional and psychological toll of staying in a failing market. Leaders often cling to hope, investing more resources in a sinking ship out of fear of admitting defeat. This section emphasizes the importance of objective analysis and data-driven decision-making, urging companies to confront reality rather than succumb to denial.

A case study of a company that waited too long to exit a failing market is

CHAPTER 2: THE ANATOMY OF A FAILING MARKET

presented, illustrating the cascading effects of delayed action. The narrative underscores the risks of inaction, including financial losses, employee layoffs, and reputational damage. It contrasts this with an example of a company that recognized the signs early and executed a graceful exit, preserving its ethical standing.

The chapter concludes with a discussion of the ethical implications of staying in a failing market. It argues that prolonging the inevitable can harm stakeholders more than an early exit, framing timely abandonment as a moral imperative rather than a failure of leadership.

4

Chapter 3: Stakeholders and the Weight of Responsibility

Every business decision affects a web of stakeholders, from employees and customers to suppliers and investors. This chapter explores the ethical responsibilities companies have to these groups when exiting a failing market. It emphasizes the importance of transparency, communication, and empathy in minimizing harm and maintaining trust.

The chapter introduces the concept of "stakeholder mapping," a tool for identifying and prioritizing the needs of different groups during an exit. It provides practical advice on how to engage with stakeholders, offering strategies for delivering difficult news and addressing concerns. The narrative stresses that how a company communicates its decision can be as important as the decision itself.

A central theme of this chapter is the idea of shared sacrifice. It argues that ethical exits require companies to distribute the burden of abandonment fairly, rather than disproportionately impacting vulnerable groups. Examples of companies that failed to do so are contrasted with those that succeeded, highlighting the long-term benefits of equitable decision-making.

The chapter also addresses the role of leadership in navigating stakeholder relationships. It calls for courage and humility, urging leaders to take responsibility for their actions and to prioritize the well-being of others

CHAPTER 3: STAKEHOLDERS AND THE WEIGHT OF RESPONSIBILITY

over their own egos.

5

Chapter 4: The Moral Case for Strategic Exits

This chapter makes a compelling argument for why strategic exits can be not only ethical but necessary. It challenges the notion that abandoning a market is inherently selfish or irresponsible, reframing it as a proactive step toward sustainability and growth.

The narrative draws on philosophical principles, such as utilitarianism and deontology, to explore the ethical dimensions of abandonment. It argues that staying in a failing market can sometimes cause more harm than good, both to the company and its stakeholders. The chapter encourages readers to think beyond traditional notions of loyalty and perseverance, advocating for a more nuanced understanding of responsibility.

A key point in this chapter is the idea of "ethical triage"—the process of making difficult decisions under pressure. It provides a framework for prioritizing actions that maximize positive outcomes while minimizing harm, offering practical guidance for leaders facing complex moral dilemmas.

The chapter concludes by emphasizing the importance of intention and execution. It argues that an exit can be ethical if it is motivated by a genuine desire to protect stakeholders and executed with care and integrity.

6

Chapter 5: Crafting an Ethical Exit Strategy

Having established the moral case for strategic exits, this chapter shifts focus to the practicalities of crafting an ethical exit strategy. It provides a step-by-step guide for planning and executing an exit that aligns with a company's values and responsibilities.

The chapter begins by outlining the key components of an ethical exit strategy, including clear communication, stakeholder engagement, and contingency planning. It emphasizes the importance of setting realistic timelines and goals, ensuring that the process is as smooth and transparent as possible.

A central theme of this chapter is the idea of "soft landings"—creating opportunities for stakeholders to transition smoothly out of the failing market. This might include offering severance packages to employees, finding alternative suppliers for partners, or providing support to customers. The narrative stresses that these efforts, while costly, are essential for maintaining trust and goodwill.

The chapter also addresses the role of leadership in executing an ethical exit. It calls for decisive action, clear communication, and unwavering commitment to the company's values. It concludes with a reminder that an ethical exit is not just about minimizing harm but also about laying the groundwork for future success.

7

Chapter 6: The Role of Communication in Ethical Exits

Communication is the cornerstone of any ethical exit. This chapter explores the importance of transparency, honesty, and empathy in delivering difficult news to stakeholders. It provides practical advice on crafting messages that are clear, compassionate, and consistent.

The chapter begins by examining common communication pitfalls, such as vague language, delayed announcements, and mixed signals. It contrasts these with examples of companies that handled their exits with grace and integrity, highlighting the long-term benefits of effective communication.

A key theme in this chapter is the idea of "radical transparency." It argues that companies should be as open as possible about their reasons for exiting a market, even when the truth is uncomfortable. The narrative emphasizes that honesty, while difficult, is essential for maintaining trust and credibility.

The chapter also addresses the emotional aspects of communication, urging leaders to acknowledge the pain and uncertainty that exits can cause. It provides strategies for showing empathy and support, such as offering resources, holding town hall meetings, and creating channels for feedback.

8

Chapter 7: The Aftermath of Abandonment

Exiting a failing market is only the beginning. This chapter explores the long-term consequences of abandonment, both for the company and its stakeholders. It emphasizes the importance of reflection, learning, and adaptation in the aftermath of an exit.

The chapter begins by examining the emotional and psychological impact of abandonment on employees, customers, and communities. It calls for companies to provide ongoing support, even after the exit is complete, to help stakeholders rebuild and move forward.

A central theme of this chapter is the idea of "ethical legacy." It argues that how a company is remembered after an exit depends not just on the decision itself but on the actions taken in its wake. The narrative encourages companies to use the experience as an opportunity for growth, learning from their mistakes and strengthening their commitment to ethical practices.

The chapter concludes with a discussion of the role of accountability in the aftermath of abandonment. It calls for companies to take responsibility for their actions, to acknowledge any harm caused, and to make amends where possible.

9

Chapter 8: Learning from Failure

Failure is an inevitable part of business, but it can also be a powerful teacher. This chapter explores how companies can learn from their experiences in failing markets, using those lessons to inform future decisions and strategies.

The chapter begins by examining the concept of "intelligent failure"—the idea that not all failures are created equal. It argues that failures can be valuable opportunities for growth, provided they are approached with the right mindset. The narrative encourages companies to embrace a culture of learning, where mistakes are seen as opportunities rather than setbacks.

A key theme in this chapter is the importance of reflection and analysis. It provides a framework for conducting post-exit reviews, identifying what went wrong, and determining how to avoid similar mistakes in the future. The narrative emphasizes the role of humility and openness in this process, urging leaders to seek feedback and learn from others.

The chapter also addresses the emotional aspects of failure, acknowledging the pain and disappointment that can accompany an exit. It provides strategies for coping with these emotions, such as seeking support, practicing self-compassion, and focusing on the lessons learned.

10

Chapter 9: Building Resilience for Future Challenges

Exiting a failing market is a test of a company's resilience. This chapter explores how companies can build the strength and flexibility needed to navigate future challenges, both ethical and practical.

The chapter begins by examining the concept of organizational resilience, defining it as the ability to adapt and thrive in the face of adversity. It provides practical advice on how to cultivate resilience, such as fostering a culture of innovation, diversifying revenue streams, and investing in employee development.

A central theme of this chapter is the idea of "ethical resilience"—the ability to maintain one's moral compass even in difficult circumstances. It argues that ethical resilience is essential for navigating the complex decisions that arise in failing markets, providing a foundation for principled action.

The chapter also addresses the role of leadership in building resilience. It calls for leaders to model resilience in their own behavior, demonstrating courage, adaptability, and a commitment to ethical principles.

11

Chapter 10: The Global Perspective on Market Exits

Market exits are not just a local phenomenon; they have global implications. This chapter explores the ethical challenges of exiting markets in different cultural, economic, and regulatory contexts.

The chapter begins by examining the unique challenges of exiting markets in developing countries, where the consequences of abandonment can be particularly severe. It calls for companies to take a more nuanced approach, considering the broader impact of their decisions on local communities and economies.

A key theme in this chapter is the idea of "global responsibility." It argues that companies have a moral obligation to consider the global implications of their actions, even when exiting a market. The narrative emphasizes the importance of cultural sensitivity, ethical consistency, and long-term thinking in navigating these complex decisions.

The chapter also addresses the role of international regulations and standards in shaping market exits. It provides practical advice on how to comply with these requirements while maintaining ethical integrity.

12

Chapter 11: The Future of Ethical Exits

As the business landscape continues to evolve, so too must our approach to ethical exits. This chapter explores emerging trends and challenges, offering insights into how companies can stay ahead of the curve.

The chapter begins by examining the impact of technology on market exits, from the rise of automation to the growing importance of data analytics. It argues that these tools can be used to make more informed and ethical decisions, provided they are applied with care and consideration.

A central theme of this chapter is the idea of "sustainable exits." It calls for companies to think beyond short-term gains, considering the long-term impact of their decisions on the environment, society, and the economy. The narrative emphasizes the importance of aligning exits with broader sustainability goals, such as reducing carbon emissions and promoting social equity.

The chapter also addresses the role of innovation in shaping the future of ethical exits. It encourages companies to experiment with new approaches, such as collaborative exits and shared-value partnerships, that prioritize the well-being of all stakeholders.

13

Chapter 12: A Call to Ethical Action

The final chapter serves as a rallying cry for ethical leadership in the face of difficult decisions. It challenges readers to embrace the principles outlined in the book, using them as a guide for navigating the complexities of market exits.

The chapter begins by summarizing the key lessons of the book, from the importance of stakeholder engagement to the value of ethical resilience. It emphasizes that ethical exits are not just a moral imperative but a strategic advantage, helping companies build trust, loyalty, and long-term success.

A central theme of this chapter is the idea of "moral courage." It calls for leaders to stand firm in their commitment to ethical principles, even when faced with pressure to prioritize profits over people. The narrative emphasizes that true leadership requires both strength and compassion, urging readers to lead with integrity and empathy.

The chapter concludes with a vision for a future where ethical exits are the norm rather than the exception. It challenges readers to be agents of change, using their influence to create a more just and sustainable business world.

14

Epilogue: The Ripple Effect of Ethical Choices

Every decision a company makes has a ripple effect, touching the lives of countless individuals and communities. This epilogue reflects on the broader impact of ethical exits, urging readers to consider the legacy they want to leave behind.

The narrative emphasizes that ethical choices are not just about avoiding harm but about creating positive change. It calls for companies to use their power and influence to make the world a better place, one decision at a time.

Book Description: The Ethics of Abandonment: Strategic Exits from Failing Markets Without Moral Collapse

In the ever-shifting landscape of business, the decision to exit a failing market is one of the most complex and morally charged challenges leaders face. *The Ethics of Abandonment* delves into the heart of this dilemma, offering a thoughtful exploration of how companies can navigate strategic exits without sacrificing their ethical integrity. This book is not just a guide for business leaders; it is a call to action for anyone who believes that profit and principle can coexist.

Through twelve compelling chapters, the book examines the multifaceted nature of market exits, from identifying the signs of a failing market to crafting an exit strategy that prioritizes the well-being of stakeholders. It

EPILOGUE: THE RIPPLE EFFECT OF ETHICAL CHOICES

challenges the notion that abandonment is inherently unethical, reframing it as a necessary and often courageous step toward sustainability and growth. Drawing on real-world examples, philosophical principles, and practical frameworks, the narrative provides a roadmap for making decisions that are both strategic and morally sound.

At its core, *The Ethics of Abandonment* is about more than just business—it is about the human impact of corporate decisions. It emphasizes the importance of empathy, transparency, and accountability, urging leaders to consider the broader consequences of their actions. From employees and customers to suppliers and communities, the book highlights the interconnected web of stakeholders who are affected by market exits and offers strategies for minimizing harm while preserving trust.

The book also looks to the future, exploring emerging trends and challenges in the global business environment. It calls for a new approach to market exits—one that aligns with broader sustainability goals and embraces innovation. By weaving together ethical theory, practical advice, and inspiring stories, *The Ethics of Abandonment* offers a vision of leadership that is both principled and pragmatic.

Ultimately, this book is a testament to the power of ethical decision-making. It challenges readers to rise above short-term pressures and embrace a long-term perspective that values people as much as profits. Whether you are a seasoned executive, an aspiring entrepreneur, or simply someone who cares about the role of business in society, *The Ethics of Abandonment* will inspire you to think deeply about the choices you make and the legacy you leave behind.

This is not just a book about how to exit a market—it is a book about how to lead with integrity in the face of difficult decisions. It is a reminder that even in the toughest moments, there is a way to act with courage, compassion, and conscience.

www.ingramcontent.com/pod-product-compliance
Lightning Source LLC
LaVergne TN
LVHW020509080526
838202LV00057B/6250